BRUSHING ETERNITY

Front, left to right: Fr Gerard Corr OSM,
Fr Alphonsus Monta OSM (Prior General), Joan Bartlett
Back, left to right: Fr Alexis Mullens OSM, Fr Vincent Naughton OSM

JOAN BARTLETT

Brushing
Eternity

Spiritual Reflections

Compiled and edited by
Teresa de Bertodano

ST PAULS

ST PAULS Publishing
187 Battersea Bridge Road
London SW11 3AS, UK

ISBN 085439 608 X

Set by TuKan DTP, Fareham, UK
Printed by Interprint Ltd, Marsa, Malta

ST PAULS is an activity of the priests and brothers
of the Society of St Paul who proclaim the Gospel
through the media of social communication

To the Servite Order

This book will bring light into our lives

Hubert Moons OSM
Prior General
The Servite Order

Contents

Acknowledgements

I am most grateful to HRH Princess Alexandra for honouring this book by writing the Foreword.

The book would not have come into being without the work of my friend Teresa de Bertodano who has compiled the text from selections of poetry and prose which I have written over the years. The book would not have been published without Teresa and I thank her very warmly.

Some of the material is taken from Conferences given to the members in formation and the professed members of the Servite Secular Institute. My thanks to the members of the Servite Secular Institute who have supported me and particularly to Dr Barbara Brosnan MBE who, as an educationalist as well as a doctor, trained so many of our aspirants to the Institute in the early days. Mary Stephens SRN has been unfailingly helpful in so many ways.

I wish to express my deep gratitude to the Servite Order and the many Friars and Sisters who have helped me over the years, including our beloved Father General, The Most Reverend Hubert Moons OSM, for his kind words of encouragement and the late Father Gerard M. Corr OSM, who has a prominent role in my simple story. My gratitude to Fr Vincent Naughton OSM, can never be adequately expressed. I would like to thank the Servite Sisters and their Mother General, Sister Felicity OSM, for their help and support over the years.

I am very grateful for the warmth and kindness I have received from the Tyburn Community, especially Mother M. Xavier McMonagle OSB, Mother General, and Mother M. Edmund Campion OSB. Through them I have deepened my love for their foundress, Mother Mary of St Peter, to whom I am indebted for her faithful help in my spiritual life.

I am grateful to Jill Morgan, who was a member of my Chelsea Red Cross detachment for many years. Also to Ann Kritzinger of Book-in-Hand for her assistance and to Annabel Robson, Commissioning Editor at St Pauls Publishing, who has been a most helpful and supportive editor.

I am grateful to Ms Kate Davies, Chief Executive of Servite Houses, for permission to use an extract from the late Cardinal Hume's Introduction to *Servite Houses 1945-89*.

I am so delighted that this book, which has been compiled by Teresa de Bertodano, has been published. It brings together an excellent collection of Joan Bartlett's work. I am sure this book will be both a comfort and an inspiration to many people.

Alexandra

From Cardinal Basil Hume's Introduction to *Servite Houses 1945–1989*

It is no accident that, in the Providence of God, the Servite Housing Association owes its foundation to Joan Bartlett, who in turn owes her achievements to a Christian commitment to the person of Christ and to His presence in those needing help and housing.

The Servite Order itself was the original source of the inspiration of the Association, through Joan Bartlett, a Servite herself, and Fr Gerard Corr OSM, a distinguished Servite Prior. The Seven Holy Founders of the Servite Order came together in 1233 because there was strife. They sought to create community where divisions existed. The early spirit of the Servite Founders still has a valid lesson for all of us.

Introduction

During the 1939–45 war I was working in London for the European Broadcasting Division of the BBC. That was my 'day' job and I did it in the face of constant bombing and the resulting office moves. Bush House in Holborn was our final destination. By night I was Commandant of a Red Cross detachment in Chelsea where I was responsible for sixty VADs (Voluntary Aid Detachments). I lodged in a room in nearby St Wilfrid's Convent and travelled to work by bicycle.

Among the volunteer staff at the Red Cross post were Caryll Houselander, Iris Wyndham and Sheila Campbell-Murdoch. Caryll was a writer and wood carver as well as being a mystic. She was to become my godmother. One day Caryll asked me if I would like to meet a friend of hers who was a Roman Catholic priest. I was not particularly interested but said that I would do so as I liked Caryll very much.

I had always belonged to the High Anglican wing of the Church of England and believed firmly in my Catholicity as an Anglo-Catholic. I had long been a disciple of John Henry Newman but had never felt any need or desire to follow him into the Roman Catholic Church.

Caryll nevertheless took me to the Servite Church of Our Lady of Dolours in the Fulham Road to meet the Servite Friar Fr Gerard Corr OSM, 'just to say "how do you do".' It was supposed to end there, but to my considerable surprise I heard myself saying that I wished to be instructed as a Roman Catholic. Caryll was amazed.

I was received into the Roman Catholic Church in 1941 and soon became a member of the Third Order or 'Tertiaries' – a group of lay people associated with the spiritual life and work of the Servite Order. I roped in a number of people from the Red Cross post to help with the typing and the Priory became a sort of off-duty rendezvous. When the bombing started we would dive under the table or make for the Lady Chapel in the Servite Church where we thought that we would be safe.

When I had been a member of the Servite Third Order for a little while I discovered that there was a rule forbidding tertiaries to bear firearms. Part of my war work involved training in the use of a rifle. Every week I used to drive down the Fulham Road and past the Servite Church en route to the rifle range. My rifle would be propped up on the seat beside me. I always hoped that one of the Friars would come out when I was driving past and see me with my rifle! But they never did.

Fr Corr was Director of Tertiaries and his work kept us very busy. At one point I displeased him over something. I cannot now remember the details. He told me that I was no longer a member of the Third Order and that when I was ready to apologise and ask for re-entry I would have to start all over again. (I don't think I was ever forbidden to help with the shorthand and typing!)

I duly began again and it was at about this time that God started to nag me. I had no idea what he was asking. The war was now drawing to a close and I was very content with my job in the European Division of the BBC. I could have been happy there for the rest of my life but I knew instinctively that this was not what God wanted.

I visited two convents, despite the fact that I was in a 'reserved occupation' and thus unable to leave my job except for a very serious reason. Entering a convent would not have been considered sufficiently serious! I was nevertheless accepted by both Religious Orders – one of them being the Servite Sisters who were teachers. Teaching wasn't for me, but the nuns said that I might be able to look after the old nuns instead. That wasn't for me either – or so I thought!

One day I returned to St Wilfrid's Convent from a bicycle ride to my parents home in Teddington to find a note from Fr Corr telling me to go round to the Servite Priory at once as he had something to say to me. I went to the Priory to be told that I was not to enter a convent but to start something 'in the world'.

I was astounded. I was due to attend a Red Cross meeting in central London shortly afterwards. Violet Markham, Head of the Government Assistance Board, began to tell us about old people wandering the streets without a home because they had lost everything in the air raids. Suddenly I knew what God had designed for my life and that he wanted me to leave all my security and happiness and find out how to take in elderly people and give them a home.

It was necessary to discover how to start a housing association, how to form a charity, how to raise money and how to find a suitable house. Our Red Cross treasurer was fond of me. He was an elderly Jewish international lawyer and had hoped that I would take up politics and become a Member of Parliament. I insisted that God wanted me to look after old people instead. 'Oppy' (Albert Oppenheimer CBE) gave me £100 – a lot of money in the 1940's – in order to register our newly formed Housing Association with the National Federation of Housing Associations (now the National Housing Federation). We were in business.

Although I had now been able to resign from the BBC I remained in touch with several colleagues including my former boss, Patrick Jubb. Patrick's father, Edwin Jubb, was Director of Navy Contracts for the Admiralty. With his help and with the assistance of an architect friend, Colonel Walter Cross, a house was found which had been in use as a hostel for Wren officers. But I had no money to buy it and so began my career of begging. I approached the Lord Mayor's Air Raid Distress Fund to be told that they did not give money for mortgages. Relying on God, I prayed to St John Bosco who had experienced similar difficulties. The Air Raid Distress Fund relented and agreed to give me £3,000. The Servite Fathers lent me £8,000 (subsequently repaid) and an American Services Fund produced a further £250. The beautiful war damaged house in The Boltons cost £11,000 and we were now able to buy it.

Despite the fact that the property had been de-requisitioned, the Wren officer in charge had failed to receive the takeover chit from the Admiralty and had only my word for the fact that the property now belonged to us. The Wrens stayed put for a further two days while I watched the bed linen which we had also purchased from the Admiralty being moved to another requisitioned property in The Boltons. Edwin Jubb at the Admiralty came to the rescue once more. The longed for takeover chit was received by the Wrens and the house was ours. I was already camping on the ground floor with a school teacher friend and our first task was to go down the road to retrieve our bed linen! The winter of 1947 was the worst in living memory and we dragged our sheets and blankets back to number 17 through heavy snow.

The Red Cross Divisional Director, Millicent Buller MBE, was another 'guardian angel'. (When I retired from Servite Houses in 1998 Millicent, then aged one hundred, travelled up from Devonshire for the occasion.) In 1947 she obtained beds and furniture for us and at long last we were able to welcome our first resident from across the Fulham Road. We used a push-barrow to wheel her possessions to The Boltons and within two weeks twenty two bombed-out elderly men and women had joined us. In four weeks we had reached our full complement of thirty two residents.

I had moved from security into the unknown and was answerable to God on the one hand and to the National Federation of Housing Associations and the Local Authority on the other. Two of the Servite Friars became members of our Management Committee although one of them, Fr McEnerney, was giving me a wide berth. Fr McEnerney was to prove a tower of strength in the future. The other Servite Committee member, Fr Corr, was packed off to Rome overnight so that he never even saw the house in The Boltons. I later discovered that there had been a suspicion in the Servite Order that I was starting 'something religious'!

One night I telephoned Fr McEnerney and asked him whether I had done anything wrong and, if not, whether some of the Servite Tertiaries could come and help me with the gruelling task of cleaning a huge house. The following day Annie Palmer arrived. Annie was a saint. She would peer at me over the top of her glasses and say 'Yes, Miss' in a voice which clearly indicated that she didn't think that I knew much. She was right.

I learned to live by the phrase 'hands that will dip in any water' and in hourly obedience to God in faith. The necessary funds always arrived – frequently at the last minute.

In 1960 it became possible to start a second house – this time in Ealing. Dr Barbara Brosnan, who was subsequently appointed MBE, joined me from the Bristol Royal Infirmary and also became one of the first members of the Servite Secular Institute. The new Servite House in Ealing broadened our base and we were now able to welcome men, women and children with severe handicaps. Barbara brought some of her nurses from Bristol including Mary Stephens, who was outstanding, and we were able to provide an extremely high standard of care.

During the same period I came into contact with Mrs Cranleigh Swash through whom we acquired a housing complex in Sydenham which took the form of self-contained flats. At the time of writing the house in The Boltons has been sold but there are hundreds of Servite dwellings throughout the country. In our fifty-plus years of existence very many people have been able to find a home with us.

From my earliest days as a Catholic I had sensed that God was calling me to a consecrated life. The call was persistent and in those days the only form of consecrated life open to women was that of a nun or religious sister. I had been all set to enter a convent when Fr Corr had told me that I was, instead, to start something 'in the world'. I had obeyed and started Servite Houses but the desire for a consecrated life persisted. It was in 1947 that the document *Provida Mater Ecclesià* was promulgated in Rome by Pope Pius XII, thus opening the way for a consecrated life lived 'in the world'.

In the same year the Servite Secular Institute was founded and in 1964 we obtained official recognition from the Holy See. The first member was Margaret Milnes Walker, and there was Vyvyenne Frost and so many others. Today we have members in many different countries, involved in all manner of occupations and living under the vows of poverty, chastity and obedience. Some, like myself, are involved in the work of Servite Houses although the majority are in other occupations. We are all united in the Servite spirit which is encapsulated in our daily prayer:

Lord Jesus, you always choose the weakest instruments for your greatest works: grant that what we have undertaken in your name and in the service of your Mother may be duly fulfilled in accordance with the desires of your heart. Teach us to be loyal and faithful to the ideals of this work and to see in everything we do the working-out of your plan and the fulfilment of your desire. Teach us so to live that we may draw many souls to you and to this Institute which your Mother has founded. Jesus, lover of souls, may we always live for you who live and reign with the Father and the Holy Spirit world without end.

Joan Bartlett OBE DSG
May 31st 2000

Father, Son and Holy Spirit

I am sometimes asked why I wrote a particular poem or piece of prose. As far as the poetry is concerned I have to say that I don't know where it comes from. It is as if God gives it to me and it is just 'there' when I come to write it down. Some of the prose is taken from talks given to members of the Secular Institute in the early days and relates to particular needs or concerns of the time.

Quite early on in the history of Servite Houses we were asked by Westminster Archdiocese to undertake the updating of the Chelsea Almshouses which are still in existence. This brought me into contact with the late Bishop Cashman who was an Assistant Bishop. One day I was telling him about my hopes for the future. When he heard about my plans for the Secular Institute he said 'This should belong to Westminster Archdiocese and I will help you.' I said 'No, my Lord, it's got to be Servite' – you didn't say 'no' to bishops in those days! Bishop Cashman did not talk to me so intimately after that but he came to see us at the Ealing house and he was a good friend to Servite Houses. I had always been convinced that the Secular Institute should belong to the Servite 'family' rather than becoming part of a diocesan structure.

His Manhood

He is God
      my Saviour
whose manhood tempers
      the irresistible force of love.

For Himself Alone

God gives himself, and we give ourselves
    to him.
His love for us is eternal, disinterested.
He loves us for our good.
He gives himself absolutely.
He loves us first and begs us to love him.

Our love must always be growing
so that the desire to please him becomes
    ever deeper.

Many good people never open the door to
loving him for himself alone,
for his own sake, rather than for his gifts.

The Everlasting Trinity

I know thee
    I know thee not at all.
Thou disturbest my soul
    yet I cannot reach out to give it to thee.

Sleep uncertain,
       body surfacing the pools:
O God, my hunger and my nothingness.

    Jesus,
let me breathe the air
    which comes down to the little pools,
touching them with eternal life.

Let me come near to the embrace
    of the everlasting Trinity

Let me, my beloved,
    let me.

Three-in-One

The God who made me, sustains me.
The Son who redeemed me
    won eternal happiness for me.
The Holy Spirit who sanctifies me
        pours out upon me his unique and
        special gifts.

The Three-in-One are constantly active
    within my soul.
God is not static within me
    like a stagnant pool.
He is the fountain of water springing
      eternally
    and ever anew within my soul.

His gifts and graces are always new.
    He gives at the exact moment I need
      his grace.
I must strive to be attentive
    to the slightest movement of the
      Blessed Trinity within.

We longed for reservation of the Blessed Sacrament in the house in The Boltons – which was unlikely to be granted to us in those pre-Vatican II days.

One day the late Bishop Craven came to visit us; he met the old people, including those ill in bed, and by the following Monday God had given us the Blessed Sacrament in our own house.

The Living Spirit

God is a person to be loved so it is perfectly natural that our footsteps should lead us to the Blessed Sacrament.

If we are out shopping it is natural that we should go into church to be with the person we love – even if we just go in for a few minutes. It isn't a duty – or even, necessarily, a pleasure. It is a sort of necessity, a kind of affinity which makes being with God the thing we desire most deeply. It is at a deeper level than, say, our tiredness or grumpiness – the fact that we don't feel up to much.

With loving God in the Blessed Sacrament, there comes adoration of the Blessed Trinity in which the spirit lives, the everlasting part of me.

Love of
Neighbour

Kindness Towards All

I have sometimes been asked to describe the 'charism' of our Institute. The dictionary tells me that the word charism refers to 'a special personal quality or power by which an individual is able to influence or inspire large numbers of people.' My reaction to that has always been 'oh dear!'. When I think of all the books I have read about people who started Religious Orders, they all seem to have had some qualification in teaching, nursing, or something of the sort. I am without qualifications and I think that the only quality I have ever had to offer is the desire to be kind. I told Our Lord that there was nothing I had in the way of qualifications but I could learn to be kind.

I think that in a special way our Institute has been characterised by kindness, by the desire to be kind one to another, and to those with whom we come into contact. In one of his books Cardinal Hume remarks that 'as priests and bishops we do most harm when we are unkind.' I think that is also true of those in consecrated religious life.

Kindness and Tact

People can spot a happy family because they sense kindness, consideration and tact. When we think of trying to serve God a bit better we need to ask ourselves whether or not we are kind and tactful – whether we are really afraid of hurting other people and really prepared to be hurt ourselves rather than cause pain to another. As we grow out of selfishness, may we also grow out of nursing our grievances and empty ourselves of our own busy-ness.

Sometimes we can think, piously, that we are doing a lot for other people, but the beginning of helping other people lies in our relationship with God. I need to be in relationship with God so that I can say 'there is nothing that separates me from my beloved.' God knows my weaknesses better than anyone else—he also knows if I am deceiving myself by pretending that the awkward things aren't there. Covering up the mouldy cake with white icing!

God Asks

After holding a number of offices in the Servite Order, St Philip Benizi became General in 1267, not because he wanted to be General but because the Order compelled him. In his travels and while making Foundations he performed many miracles. When the poor starving Friars had nothing to eat, bread arrived on the table!

Best of all I love the miracle of the leper who asked for alms. St Philip had no money, but he had an undertunic and gave it away. The leper was cured. Would we be able to take our clothes and give them away? Would we be able to touch a dirty leprous person without recoiling? God asks a lot of those who are dearest to him.

Christ in My Neighbour

When I was sixteen I started work as a secretary in London while still living with my family in Teddington where I was the eldest of three daughters. In my spare time I was captain of a Girl Guide troop and I remember being with the Guides one beautiful summer evening when one of the parish curates joined us and started to talk about confession: not compulsory in the Church of England and seldom spoken of in some churches. What the curate said affected me tremendously. Should I go to confession? What if my mother found out? I would be punished by someone who was upright, hardworking for her children, very caring but moulded in the pattern of the Victorian era. Mother had an absolute hatred of 'papists'.

I wanted to discover all kinds of things for myself in a way that came out as 'half for you, Lord, and half for me.' I went to confession and I was found out! As an Anglo-Catholic I started going to Mass on weekdays – even worse! My mother said I was only doing it to get out of cleaning the grates and helping her in the house before I went to work. But when I tried staying at home I found it made no difference. I had become separated from the family and was beginning to measure my life against what I thought Jesus wanted.

Later on when I had become a Roman Catholic, one of the Servite Friars, Fr Corr, used to come and visit my mother and they became great friends.

Swept up into God

Jesus draws the soul away from its little
     kingdoms.
Unhindered by time or other considerations
    it is swept up into God.
We are not able to choose when this state
     comes to us.
It may be after we are particularly sorry
    for something we have done.
It may be after we have striven for him
    in a variety of circumstances.
But I do not think it could ever come to
     anybody
    who was not aware of Christ in their
    neighbour first.

Charity

In the green leaf from the tree
    hiding itself 'neath the
    carpet of autumn.

In the old organ grinder
    raising his hat for the dead
    and the closed eyes of the sick child
    who, awake, sleeps
    for the peace of its mother,
    there is charity.

In the exquisite simplicity of devotion,
    and the care of the sick
    as caring for God.

In the hands that will dip in any water
    lieth charity.

It is the mystery of marriage
    and of a nun who lives to worship God.

It covers up the weariness of heaven
    indeed, it is heaven,

      for it is Love.

Serving Others

I have always had a great devotion to St John Bosco who did so much to improve the lot of boys and young men in nineteenth century Italy. His feast day falls on 31st January and although I can no longer remember in which year this was, I know that it was on the Feast of St John Bosco during the 1950's that we received a letter from Southern Africa 'out of the blue' asking if the Institute could provide medical staff to help two doctors to start a hospital in Swaziland. How had they discovered our little Institute? The 'coincidence' of the dates convinced me that St John Bosco had had a hand in it!

Dr Barbara Brosnan and Dity von Spaun SRN went out with Marlene Sach SRN. Dity and Marlene have spent most of their lives working with the Servite Friars in Africa, first in Swaziland and then in Zululand when we had a request to start a similar undertaking there. In the early days there was no money to pay salaries so we financed the work from England. But that has all changed now. I have been to visit Swaziland and Zululand and have been enormously moved by the love and devotion which goes into the work there.

Cost What May

We have only to read the life of someone like the Curé d'Ars or St John Bosco to see what determination means. Nothing deflected the Curé from his purpose. He set out to do something and he did it – no matter what people said. He refused whatever comforts or 'lesser things' were offered him because God was his horizon, his vision. Souls were his harvest and nothing ever put him aside from his purpose.

St John Bosco was the same about children and we can be thankful for his Religious Order, the Salesians, and their schools. All this because one person made up his mind to carry out his purpose at whatever cost.

Helping Hand

One day a serious epidemic of flu obliged us to close our doors in The Boltons. The doctor told us that nobody should come in or go out. That was impossible! Our neighbour Lady Craigmyle offered to help me and we scrubbed and polished.

The Craigmyles were wonderful friends to us and our summer sales were always held in their delightful garden.

United to Him

If life does not seem to include suffering of any kind, if it all appears easy – we need to be suspicious. Suffering and loving God go together. If we love someone we suffer for them and with them, and it is exactly the same with loving God. That is why the saints, coming nearer and nearer to God, took on voluntary suffering to make sure that they were united to him.

We need to do the simple things – ordinary, everyday kindnesses. 'High powered penance operators' don't necessarily go to God first. It is rather the simple, kindly person, always at the disposal of everyone, full of God, without duplicity.

We need to be absolutely natural and to ensure that there is nothing in us which is artificial or a pose.

Our Lady and the Saints

God's Plan

I often wonder why God called me in this particular way, called me to be a Servite – a Servant of Mary. When people talk about vocation I sometimes long to say 'I can tell you!', but I don't because not everybody wants to know that vocation is a distinct calling from God. It really is. It really happens. I was called to look after old people. You may be called in some other way. God has his own plan for each one of us.

Everlasting Waters

I hear the sound of everlasting waters
   brushing eternity
   and in the air there is the breath
   of eternal spring.

Behold, a soul approaches heaven,
   her feet touching the paths of obedience
   where the reaper cannot come
   with the sickle of death.

How beautiful she is in her garments of
      poverty
   and, as the rags touch the earth,
   Jesus is born again in new grain.

Pure Love

The saints were 'eaten up' with love of God and we can be 'eaten up' in the same way if we make the effort. We do not always have to feel that we want to do everything for God. Sometimes we are tired or strained through overwork – physically not up to the mark. Sometimes we are tempted to distaste or revulsion. But charity is a matter of the will and not solely of the emotions so we need to try to rise above ourselves and to love God.

The Divine Fire

Sorrow knows nothing, only her sorrow.
    She is unconscious of the noise and
        the cold –
    of the voices of men and the passing
        footstep.
She only wants to look at Him
    until death removes the understanding
        from His eyes.

Where are we standing?
    Very near.
The wind rustles her garments –
    so near.
Her breath comes and goes –
    nearer
Your will is broken,
    you cannot run away now.
You have become a spark from the divine fire
    you will stay until the end.

Coldness and Disdain

When Our Lord showed his Sacred Heart to St Margaret Mary, he showed her the wonder of his love for us and the ingratitude he received in return. He told her that ingratitude and disdain were more hurtful to him than anything else that he suffered during his Passion. If only, he said, they would give me a little love in return, I would count as little all that I had done for them and would, were it possible, do more. But they meet all my efforts with coldness and disdain.

The Calling

Since the earliest days of what was to become the Secular Institute I had been convinced that the call to the Religious Life had nothing to do with the level of education. One of my early horrors was when Fr Corr told me that Barbara Brosnan was better educated than me and that her pronunciation was better than mine! As a result I disliked Barbara, in fact we disliked each other! We did our best to try to get along and ended up by becoming firm friends which we have remained to this day.

It was the calling that mattered – the conviction that God had called us with many others to become part of a single religious family.

Keep Trying

Am I trying to be really humble? What does it cost me, for instance, to see someone managing far better than I do and with many more graces while I just go on trying. Not trying to be first but trying to please God. A vocation is not necessarily given by Our Lord to the person with the most virtues, but to the person who is determined to conquer her faults and to go on trying to conquer irritability, laziness, bad temper, attacks against faith etc.

We are greatly helped by reading the lives of the saints. In not one saint can we see a person without trials. There were trials in the saint's own deficiencies of character, in getting on with other people – making allowances for the other person. All the saints and good people we know have one thing in common. They go on trying. Just that and nothing else.

Fixed in Heaven

In him there is no comeliness –
    he has trodden the winepress alone
    and there is no man with him.
He is untidy, shattered, disfigured and bent –
    the sweat is on his forehead – the beads
        of death.
But love is supreme
    because love is the everlasting now.

She, the woman, leaps forward
    and Jesus looks up and sees his mother
    and in that look is the perfection
of everything they have shared together
    from the moment she conceived him in
        her womb,
    everything they have built up together.
In her heart is the unquenchable love of
        a mother,
    supreme in its attraction
    towards the unquenchable love of a son.

Only a look, yes,
　　but that look contains the depths of
　　understanding
　　and her heart is all his.
She is sensitive to his suffering
　　as only a mother can be.

They look into one another's eyes
　　and that look is forever fixed in heaven.

Everlasting Joy

With the Father and the Spirit
   the adorable Son welcomed his mother
      into heaven
because she was consumed with love
   – and Jesus came to meet her.

Mary is taken up with her Son.
   She who had shared the hurt in his eyes
      when his children wounded him
now shares his look of everlasting joy.

Prayer

Christ in Me

The Old Testament and the Psalms can be a wonderful help to prayer. Many passages from the Prophets can raise the mind and the heart to God.

In the New Testament we see and hear God working and speaking to us in his humanity. The words of Christ are the words of God. The miracles of Christ are the miracles of God. As St John tells us, God is tabernacled among us. All that Christ says and does, God says and does. He is truth, without any shade of deceit. We read of his love and his tenderness, of his promises which will never be broken.

If we meditate upon the Gospels, the words and actions of God dwelling within us, and if we strive to have the mind of Christ within us, then we can truly say with St Paul: 'I live: no, not I, but Christ lives in me' (Gal 2.20).

Ways of Prayer – 1

The simplest way to start to pray is through vocal prayer. We use the thoughts and feelings of another person and we begin to dwell on what we are saying.

A bit further on we come to meditation. We have a set pattern to guide us and we pass methodically from one consideration to another, developing our subject. We make resolutions and reason predominates rather than the affections.

Later on in meditation we may find that the affections take first place – joy, thanksgiving, praise, adoration of God.

Ways of Prayer – 2

Finally, in the ordinary ways of prayer, we have the prayer of simple regard or simplicity in which it is sufficient for the soul to put itself into the presence of God. Although the prayer of simplicity can give the impression of simple repose of mind and heart, this is not in fact the case. The contemplative, in the fixity of her regard, requires all her powers of adhesion, if only to protect herself from allowing her mind to wander.

No Mainspring

We have all, at sometime or another, held something very beautiful in our hands: a beautiful watch, for example. But if the mainspring is broken nothing happens when you try to wind it up.

That is a life without prayer. What we do may appear very beautiful, but without prayer we have no mainspring and grace cannot flow into us. Underneath the outward show our lives are meaningless. St Thomas Aquinas tells us that the efficient cause of devotion is meditation or contemplation on our side: and devotion is an act of the will in ready service of God.

Love is the Pendulum

There are no limits to which one person will not go for another in real earthly love which finds its value in action rather than words. And this is also the case in the realm of the spirit. The love of God for the soul and of the soul for God has no limits either. Prayer is in the will and in the look, and not necessarily in speech. Love is the pendulum which by day and by night binds the soul to Our Lord in charity – which is love. From that vantage point we may glimpse what God does not permit us to understand in this life – the eternal charity flowing from the Blessed Trinity.

Joy

Holiness does not mean that we are 'dry', lacking in fun, uptight. Some genuinely holy religious people I have known have been so narrow, so lacking in joy – as if they feel that joy has no place in worship.

Joy *is* part of God. It *is* part of worship. If joy is missing from our lives we need to stop and see what has gone wrong. Love of God not only brings joy to ourselves – and that is important – but it brings joy to other people.

Light and Shade

Those who have come very close to Jesus in their life of prayer have some of his love burned into their hearts. In order to preserve that love they are willing to forgive even a big injury.

Suffering and joy are the light and shade on the path to heaven. The perfect balance lies in both: lies in the acceptance of God's will, in the bending of our hearts and minds under the corrective measures God takes in order to make us realise that this life is not our final goal.

Love in Action

Bishop Craven was a dear bishop and a great friend to us. For many years he allowed us to beg for funds outside his church in London, St James's, Spanish Place. His sister, who also became our friend, used to give us hot drinks as the hours wore on. We took every opportunity for begging.

Quite recently I was standing on Clapham Common shaking a tin when a woman came up to me and asked what I was collecting for. I told her that we were at that time collecting for homeless people. She told me that she never gave money to help homeless people and I was shocked.

Giving and Receiving

When we talk to our friends we do not use long formal sentences, we simply tell them what we feel and think – sometimes, indeed, when the friendship is very close, words are not necessary – just the fact of being there is all that matters. The love of a friend for a friend flows between them in companionable silence.

We can be like this with God, telling him that we love him, asking him to help us when a difficult piece of work comes along. Sometimes we need only give a look of love – to think the name of 'Jesus'. We can share our problems with God, ask him to guide us to do the right thing; seek his advice. But it's no good deciding on a course of action and then asking God to agree. Prayer is for giving and receiving – as in all human friendship.

When we truly love we are, by the very nature of our love, compelled to give. The more we pray, the more we *want* to pray because God is continually pouring the grace of prayer and the longing for prayer into our hearts.

The Journey
to God

A Consecrated Life

When we first started the Servite Secular Institute our leaders were treated as religious superiors and we had several practices which were reminiscent of a convent! The house in The Boltons was a sort of headquarters for us and if you came into Mass late you had to kneel in the aisle beside the Superior – in the early days it was me! We had one silly practice which was that we all wore dark blue cardigans so that we looked the same – but we weren't meant to be nuns and gradually we became our natural selves.

I remember Bishop Cashman asking me, as a consecrated religious, how I would behave if I was at a reception. I replied that I would behave in a normal way; take a drink, speak about ordinary things – and be careful to be up to date in everyday knowledge.

Longing for Jesus

I know what longing is
    stark, craving longing for Jesus
the body leaning forward and absorbing
       nothing,
    arms moving, moving to catch nothing.
The mind coming out of its cells, looking...
    going into its cells, searching
    yet finding nothing, nothing.

Then the soul finding Jesus in its
       communion
and losing him again
    as contact with the world makes us
       lose him
so that every part of me aches for him again.

Who is Myself?

Who has hidden my soul?
    Is it hanging on wood
chiselled about by man?
    or is it myself?

The sea races in
    over the pools
where there has always been water
    and I know not their depth.

Who is myself?
    I cannot answer.

Sharing

Richard Castillo was my doctor and as the number of Servite Houses increased he insisted that I must learn to drive and get a car. The money had to be found for the lessons – it's hard to be a pauper! I learnt to drive and to my relief passed my test at the first attempt.

One sad day Dr Castillo was murdered in Chelsea and his murderer was never brought to justice. Dr Castillo's widow, Bobby, shared my life for many years after this tragic event and was such a support to me in the work of Servite Houses. We used to organise the Alexandra Rose Day collections together and the money from our collection 'pitch' did a lot to help us to keep going.

Purification

Anyone who tries to do something for God seems to come up against it quite quickly. God can, indeed, appear to be misleading us. We thought that we were doing what he wanted but it all seems to be going wrong. In the early stages of the Religious Life it is usual to be filled with fervour and we often receive a sort of foretaste of heaven. We see the banner, we hear the marching of countless other men and women going in the same direction and we are proud of our association with the heavenly army. We say to ourselves 'This is for me and I will not be separated from it'.

Then God removes himself: a chosen friend departs, our best laid plans go awry, we don't feel well. Suddenly 'the world' reappears with all its attractions. God seems to be absent so there is nothing but 'the world'. It is during these periods that our patience demonstrates our vocation and we are purified.

The Adorable God

Between the soul and the tabernacle
    lies the road that knows no living thing
where there is neither heat nor shade,
    light nor darkness
and no distinction of colour or form.

In this I plunge forwards
    into the nothingness
        of the adorable God.

No Turning Back

So many things have happened to us, some of them good, others bad. Some things we wish to remember and others we would willingly obliterate for ever. Sometimes we would not have been able to hold on had it not been for the outstretched hand of a servant of God. At other times there was no help available and we failed through our own weakness or lack of vision.

But ahead of us and on all sides there is uncharted territory and we are going into it in order to discover that 'He hath indeed made all things new' (Rev 21:5). Once we have been called by God and have responded there is no turning back. We can never again say that we do not understand the purpose of our life. The good servant, like the good housewife, turns everything to good account.

No One Will Know

I have wounded my beloved
and I cannot bear it.
> I am proud. I despise my sins
> they are beneath me.

When I have said I am sorry
I will rush away.
> When it is evening I will stay
> outside the family circle.

It doesn't matter. It doesn't matter.
I will work very hard.
> I will keep Jesus at arm's length.
> I won't sin again

and I shall be the same as others
> no one will know.

Jesus and Eternity

Without the unspoken consciousness of Jesus and eternity the mind is swept from one thing to another. We find ourselves occupied over and over again with the virtues or otherwise of the people we are with: small talk, the 'fors' and 'againsts' of this or that and, worst of all, the introspection which always comes with uncertain service of God.

If we don't really know what we are doing, or why we are doing it, we cloud our perspective. We go into ourselves and round and about. We think about nothing but ourselves. This leads to trouble, disappointment and the failure to go on trying. We need to leave ourselves to God a bit more – to become as the arrow from the bow of a good archer – straight and clean with our minds fixed on Jesus and on eternity.

My Rags, My Heart

Jesus took my arms
    and put them each side of me
    and then told me to look at him.
As I looked, I saw his beautiful heart
    beating through his flesh.
He just put out his arms
    and took me.
No one saw
    and no one but he heard what I said.
He held me very close and melted my heart
    and I loved him more
        than I had ever loved him before.

As he held me
    he had his arms round my rags
        as well as my heart.

Death
and Eternity

Comfort the Dying

Many years ago I was taken into the old St Stephen's Hospital in the Fulham Road because my asthma was making breathing very difficult. I wasn't allowed to get out of bed. The patient in the bed opposite was obviously very ill. I wondered why there wasn't anybody sitting with her. Suddenly she threw up her arms and then fell back. She was dead. Doctors and nurses came running from everywhere. The curtains were drawn around her and she was whisked away on a stretcher. No prayers, nothing. Just a poor old woman. I wrote this prayer in her memory and I say it every day.

O Blessed Trinity
someone will die today, neglected;
perhaps a young person,
        perhaps an old;
perhaps in a hospital ward,
        perhaps at home.

I beg you to accept my prayer,
so that the departing soul does not come
            before you
unloved and uncared for
    in our natural world.

Especially I would beg of you
to take my prayer to help some old person
who dies with no one to share
the thought of eternity,
    the journey;
with no one to help the
    bewildered soul
    in its last agony.

Please bless us, O Lord,
and all we are trying to do,
and comfort the dying –
    in all death's circumstances.

Brushing Eternity

Intensity, deepening in intensity.
   In the cool grey walls, silence.
     In the human heart
        silence and adoration.

   Behold, I have lost my being,
   I have brushed eternity.

The Will of God

The Belgian Trappist monk, Michael Carlier, was called up in 1914 to take part in the Great War. As he knelt under a torrential downpour in the middle of the road, waiting for the bus to take him away from all that he loved, his Abbot said to him 'Be a good soldier, never forget that sanctity consists in the entire accomplishment of the will of God in one's own regard at any given moment.'

This monk loved his Order above all things. He became a soldier (under compulsion) and was killed in battle. He kept his Rule and in the rumble of fearful battle, in the mess rooms and while fighting alongside soldiers, he never lost that heavenly privilege of contemplating heaven and contemplating God. A well trained soldier of Christ and a well trained soldier for his earthly country.

Road to Holiness

The distinguished Canadian soldier and statesman Georges Vanier wrote, 'In our era the road to holiness necessarily passes through the world of action.' General Vanier's early life was marked by four years spent in the trenches during the First World War followed by a successful diplomatic career which culminated in his appointment as Governor General of Canada (1959-67). At the end of an extremely active and successful life General Vanier was so far advanced along the road to holiness that the question of his beatification is now being seriously considered.

Few of us are called to live on the public stage but most of us are obliged to live lives of increasing 'busyness'. God meets us 'where we are' rather than where we might wish to be. There is no 'ideal' path to heaven and the most perfect way of life that any of us can embrace is the one to which God calls us.

Restless Waters

And now O Lord I hear the everlasting waters
    brushing your eternal stronghold
An unbreathèd wind moves by your helpless
      daughter
    and takes her in the last deep fold.

And, in the first strange hush, the friendless
      weanèd spirit
    laps idly in her airless sphere
till Jesus bids sweet hope forerunnèd joy
      to give it
    and pity sheds a wingèd tear.

And now again I hear the restless waters
      pounding
    the fort where death cannot prevail,
and something bids me on, though fear is
      still retarding
    my entrance to reveal my tale.

One heart, one beat, one name, O Christ, my
      God, your glory,
    in chasmèd deep eternal love.
One look, I know the cost, those marks,
      I know the story,
    the cost of life with thee above.

Into This Place

Down in the slime of the trenches men waited. Here and there light came through the rain soaked roof. Their guns were silenced, their limbs frozen. If a shell burst overhead they would be helpless.

As the priest elevated the chalice the groans of the injured formed the only note of praise. And Jesus came into this place which was the best that men had to offer him: into the stench of urine and faeces. A blinded man pressed his face into the mud. He said to Jesus: 'I know you are here in this place and I wish we were clean to receive you. I am done for now. I can't serve you again. But at least I can love you.'

Requiem

If God revived the dead and sent them back
    would they come, half-memoried with
        another world?
Looking beyond their beloved
    like fog wraiths in the bracken,
passing their fingers through
    the damp in the hills.
        Shrouded in eternity.
        Puzzled without eternity.

Would they whisper through the wind to
        the gulls
    and laugh at their calling through the
      sea's surge
      reaching to catch them
    frightened at catching nothing?

Would they remember,
    and ask God to take them back?

Children of God

I have always believed that we are all children of God, whatever our denomination or religion and I always insisted that the question of religion should play no part in the admittance policy of Servite Houses. Although it was frowned on by the Catholic Church in the 1950's, I have always attended the funerals of members of our 'family', whatever their place of worship.

Flashlight on God

It takes far more preparation and patience to prepare ourselves for heaven than to prepare ourselves for the hardest examination in a subject in which we are interested. For those who have caught a glimpse of the loveliness of God, and of his reality, our preparation for heaven requires that we work towards a state of life in which everything is God. A life in which prayer is work and work is prayer. A life in which our friends reflect God to us and we are a 'flashlight on God' for them.

We need to discard all that is unnecessary in order to pursue that which is most real: an intense and absolute union with God.

Appointment with Jesus

So shall my soul
   break through this chastened flesh.
And, with some final struggling,
   (in courtesy to nature)
keep an appointment
   earlier made with Jesus.